W9-COF-200

A Grassland Habitat

Kelley MacAulay and Bobbie Kalman

Crabtree Publishing Company

www.crabtreebooks.com

Created by Bobbie Kalman

Dedicated by Nancy Johnson
For my Mom and my Grandma, the two most impressive and influential women in my life.

Editor-in-Chief
Bobbie Kalman

Writing team
Kelley MacAulay
Bobbie Kalman

Substantive editor
Kathryn Smithyman

Editors
Molly Aloian
Michael Hodge
Rebecca Sjonger

Design
Katherine Kantor
Margaret Amy Salter (cover)
Samantha Crabtree (series logo)

Production coordinator
Heather Fitzpatrick

Photo research
Crystal Foxton

Special thanks to
Jack Pickett and Karen Van Atte

Illustrations
Barbara Bedell: pages 17, 32 (top)
Katherine Kantor: pages 26-27, 32 (middle)
Margaret Amy Salter: pages 12, 15, 24, 32 (bottom)

Photographs
iStockphoto.com: Rob Freeman: title page; Laura Oconnor:
    page 17 (bottom left); Allen Thornton: page 11
Visuals Unlimited: Joe McDonald: page 18; Dr. William J. Weber: page 29
Minden Pictures: Jim Brandenburg: pages 13, 19
Other images by Adobe Image Library, Corbis, Corel, Creatas,
    Digital Vision, Eyewire, and Photodisc

Library and Archives Canada Cataloguing in Publication
MacAulay, Kelley
    A grassland habitat / Kelley MacAulay & Bobbie Kalman.
(Introducing habitats)
Includes index.
ISBN-13: 978-0-7787-2959-4 (bound)
ISBN-13: 978-0-7787-2987-7 (pbk.)
ISBN-10: 0-7787-2959-1 (bound)
ISBN-10: 0-7787-2987-7 (pbk.)
    1. Grassland ecology--Juvenile literature. I. Kalman, Bobbie, date.
II. Title. III. Series.

QH541.5.P7M32 2006   j577.4   C2006-904097-4

Library of Congress Cataloging-in-Publication Data
MacAulay, Kelley.
    A grassland habitat / Kelley MacAulay & Bobbie Kalman.
        p. cm. -- (Introducing habitats)
    ISBN-13: 978-0-7787-2959-4 (rlb)
    ISBN-10: 0-7787-2959-1 (rlb)
    ISBN-13: 978-0-7787-2987-7 (pb)
    ISBN-10: 0-7787-2987-7 (pb)
    1. Grassland ecology--Juvenile literature. I. Kalman, Bobbie. II. Title.

QH541.5.P7M328 2006
577.4--dc22
                                          2006018784

Crabtree Publishing Company

www.crabtreebooks.com   1-800-387-7650

Published in Canada
Crabtree Publishing
616 Welland Ave.
St. Catharines, ON
L2M 5V6

Published in the United States
Crabtree Publishing
PMB16A
350 Fifth Ave., Suite 3308
New York, NY 10118

Published in the United Kingdom
Crabtree Publishing
White Cross Mills
High Town, Lancaster
LA1 4XS

Published in Australia
Crabtree Publishing
386 Mt. Alexander Rd.
Ascot Vale (Melbourne)
VIC 3032

Contents

What is a habitat?

A **habitat** is a place in nature.
Plants live in habitats. Animals
live in habitats, too. Some
animals make homes in habitats.

Living and non-living things

There are **living things** in habitats. Plants and animals are living things. There are also **non-living things** in habitats. Rocks, water, and dirt are non-living things.

living thing

non-living thing

Everything they need

Plants and animals need air, water, and food to stay alive. They have everything they need in their habitats. This ground squirrel found food to eat in its habitat.

A habitat home

Some animals have homes. Their homes are in their habitats. This badger's home is under the ground. The badger sleeps in its home.

7

Grassland habitats

Grasslands are habitats. They are open, flat areas of land. Many plants grow in grasslands. Most of the plants are grasses. There are very few trees in grasslands.

Grasslands called prairies

This book is about grasslands called **prairies**. Prairies are found in Canada and the United States. Plants and animals live in the prairies. These bison live in the prairies.

Prairie weather

There are four **seasons** in the prairies. The seasons are spring, summer, autumn, and winter. Strong winds blow on the prairies in every season. This deer is resting on the prairie grass in spring.

Changing weather

The weather in the prairies changes as the seasons change. Spring is warm. Some rain falls. Summer is hot. Many prairie plants grow in summer. Autumn is cool. Prairie plants begin to die. Winter is cold. Snow falls on the prairies.

Prairie plants

purple coneflower

Most prairie plants are grasses. The grasses are often tall. They sway in the wind. Flowers grow on some prairie plants. Daisies and purple coneflowers are prairie plants that have flowers.

yellow daisies

Long, strong roots

In prairies, there are no hills to block the wind. How do plants stay in the ground? Prairie plants have long roots. The long roots grow deep down in the ground. The roots hold the prairie plants in place as the wind blows.

Plants make food

Living things need food to stay alive. Plants make their own food. They use sunlight, air, and water to make food. Making food from sunlight, air, and water is called **photosynthesis**.

Parts for making food

A plant gets sunlight through its leaves. It also gets air through its leaves. The plant gets water through its roots. The plant uses sunlight, air, and water to make food.

Leaves take in air.

Leaves take in sunlight.

Roots take in water from the soil.

Prairie animals

eagle

Many animals live in the prairies. They find food in the prairies. They also find places to live. Which prairie animals have you seen before?

prairie dog

pronghorn

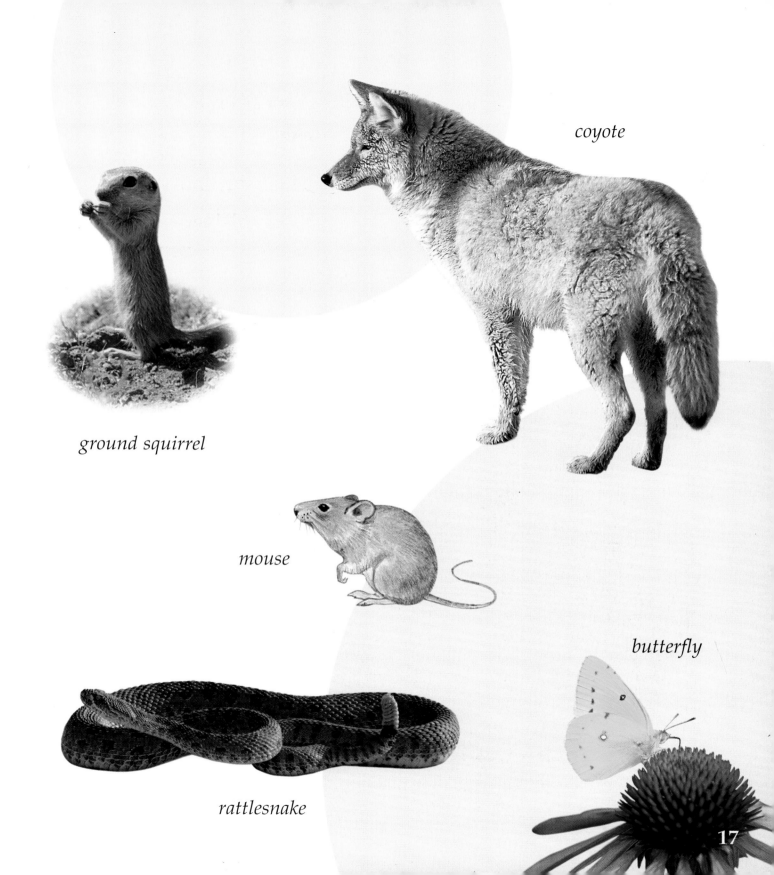

coyote

ground squirrel

mouse

butterfly

rattlesnake

17

Prairie water

There are **streams** flowing through prairies. Streams have **shallow**, moving water. Shallow water is not deep. Fish swim in the streams. This mink caught a fish to eat.

Prairie potholes

In prairies, there are wide holes filled with water. These holes are called **prairie potholes**. Prairie potholes have shallow water. Bull rushes and reeds are plants that grow in prairie potholes.

Pothole animals

Many birds live around prairie potholes. Ducks and geese live around prairie potholes. The birds swim in the water. They eat plants that grow in water.

Using water

Many other animals visit prairie potholes. They drink the water. They eat the plants in the water. Animals walk in the water on hot summer days. The water cools off their warm bodies. This elk is cooling off in a prairie pothole.

Finding food

Animals must eat food to stay alive. Some animals are **herbivores**. Herbivores eat only plants. Prairie dogs are herbivores. They eat grasses.

Meat-eaters

Some animals are **carnivores**. Carnivores eat other animals. Badgers are carnivores. They eat prairie dogs, ground squirrels, and birds.

Eating many foods

Some animals are **omnivores**.
Omnivores eat both plants and other
animals. This red fox is an omnivore.
It eats fruit, mice, and rabbits.

Getting energy

sun

All living things need **energy** to grow and to move. Energy comes from the sun. Plants get energy from the sun. Animals must eat other living things to get energy. A rabbit is a herbivore. It gets energy by eating grasses.

grasses

rabbit

Energy for carnivores

A carnivore gets energy by eating other animals. A hawk is a carnivore. It gets energy by eating a rabbit.

hawk

Underground homes

Some prairie animals dig homes under the ground. Prairie dogs dig underground homes called **towns**. Towns have many rooms. The rooms are joined by tunnels. Ground squirrels also dig large homes. The squirrels run into their homes when other animals come close.

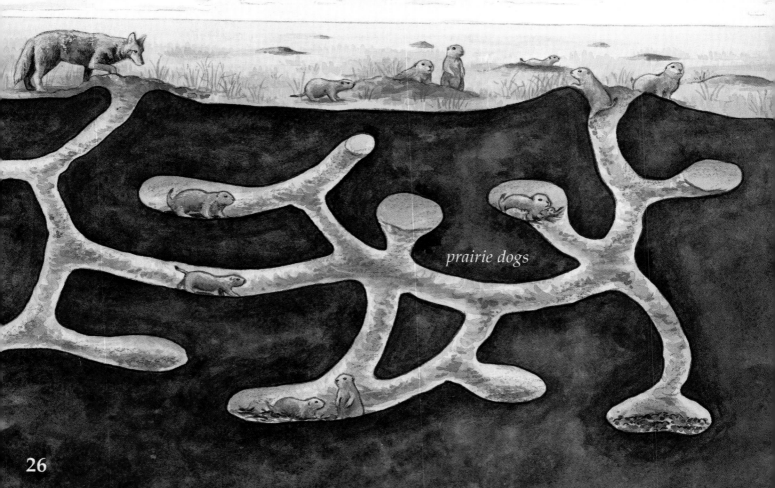

prairie dogs

Living in towns

When prairie dogs make new towns, other animals move into the old towns. Ferrets and badgers live in old prairie dog towns. The prairie dogs no longer live in these homes.

ground squirrels

ferret

badger

Safer at night

Some prairie animals come out of their homes only at night. It is safer for the animals to come out at night than it is for them to come out during the day. In the dark, the animals can hide more easily from other animals. This black-footed ferret comes out at night.

Night mice

Grasshopper mice sleep during the day.
They sleep in homes under the ground.
They wake up and come out of their
homes at night to look for food. They
eat mainly grasshoppers and other mice.

Hard to see

Some prairie animals are hard to see, even during the day! This ground squirrel has stripes on its back and head. The stripes look like the long grasses. Other animals may not see the ground squirrel standing in the grasses.

The same color

This bobcat has brown fur with dark spots. The grasses around the bobcat are also brown. There are dark areas in the grasses. The bobcat blends in with the grasses.

Words to know and Index

animals
pages 4, 5, 6, 7, 9,
16-17, 20, 21, 22, 23,
24, 25, 26, 27, 28, 30

habitats
pages 4, 5, 6, 7, 8

energy
pages 24-25

food
pages 6, 14, 15, 16,
22-23, 29

hiding
pages 30-31

homes
pages 4, 7, 26-27, 28, 29

plants
pages 4, 5, 6, 8, 9,
11, 12-13, 14, 15, 19,
20, 21, 22, 23, 24

seasons
pages 10, 11

Other index words
carnivores 22, 25
herbivores 22, 24
living things 5, 14, 24
non-living things 5
omnivores 23
photosynthesis 14
water 5, 6, 14, 15,
18-19, 20, 21

1 2 3 4 5 6 7 8 9 0   Printed in the U.S.A.   5 4 3 2 1 0 9 8 7 6